TENNESSEE VOICES ANTHOLOGY

2018-2019

THE POETRY SOCIETY OF TENNESSEE

A Member of the National Federation of State Poetry Societies

Editorial Board
Florence Bruce
JoAn Howerton
Janet Qually
Lori Goetz

Copyright © 2019 The Poetry Society of Tennessee

All rights reserved. No part of this publication may be reproduced, distributed, or transmitted in any form or by any means, including photocopying, recording, or other electronic or mechanical methods, without the prior written permission of the publisher, except in the case of brief quotations embodied in critical reviews and certain other noncommercial uses permitted by copyright law.

ISBN: 978-1-951300-95-1

www.tnpoetry.org

Cover is the Original Painting of William Hill

Published by Liberation's Publishing LLC
www.liberationspublishing.com

TENNESSEE VOICES ANTHOLOGY

2018-2019

THE POETRY SOCIETY OF TENNESSEE

A Member of the National Federation of State Poetry Societies

Editorial Board
Florence Bruce
JoAn Howerton
Janet Qually
Lori Goetz

Contents

OFFICERS AND COMMITEES 6

Past Presidents 9

The History Of The Poetry Society Of Tennessee 11

Poets Laureate 12

Honorary Members 13

The 2018 Mid-South Poetry Festival 14

Winners of the Monthly Contest 17

Patron Poems 29

Winners of Festival Poems 39

Student Winners 79

The Eye Poem 85

OFFICERS AND COMMITEES

OFFICERS PST-MEMPHIS 2019-2020

President - JoAn Howerton

Vice-President - Russell Strauss

Corresponding/Recording Secretary - Lori Goetz

Treasurer - Janet Qually

Director - Janet Qually

Director - William Hill

Parliamentarian - Frances Cowden

Northeast Branch President - Rose Klix

Knoxville Branch President - Sharon Fox

COMMITTEE CHAIRPERSONS PST-MEMPHIS 2019-20

CONTESTS - Ann Carolyn Cates

PUBLICATIONS - Nicole Mangum

PST WEBSITE - Lori Goetz/Kellie Clelland

PROGRAM CO-CHAIRS
Russell Strauss/Lori Goetz/Florence Bruce/Frances Cowden

STUDENT CONTESTS - Frances Cowden

MID-SOUTH POETRY FESTIVAL (2019)
Director - JoAn Howerton

Contest Chair - Lori Goetz

ASSISTANTS TO FESTIVAL DIRECTOR
Janet Qually and William Hill

OFFICERS PST-MEMPHIS 2018-2019

President - JoAn Howerton

Vice-President - Russell Strauss

Corresponding/Recording Secretary - Lori Goetz

Treasurer - Leslie Blakeburn

Director - Frances Cowden

Director - William Hill

Parliamentarian - Randy Stoker

Northeast Branch President - Rose Klix

Knoxville Branch President - Sharon Fox

COMMITTEE CHAIRPERSONS PST-MEMPHIS 2018-19

CONTESTS
J. Pompford "Pete" Harris/Florence Bruce
PUBLICATIONS - William H. King

PST WEBSITE - William H. King

PROGRAMS - Leslie Blakeburn

STUDENT CONTESTS - Frances Cowden

MID-SOUTH POETRY FESTIVAL (2018)

Director - JoAn Howerton

Contest Chair - Lori Goetz

Assistants to Festival Director
Janet Qually and William Hill

Officers PST NE 2019-2020

President - Rose Klix

Vice-President - Calvin Ross

Treasurer/Membership/Facebook - Howard Carman

Secretary: Jan Barnett (resigned due to health); Connie Mohr (started May 2019)

Committee Chairpersons 2018-2019

Webmaster - J. Michael Ramey

Newsletter/Publicity - Judith Donley

Contest Chair: Carolyn Lilly ((resigned due to health) currently vacant

Critique meeting - Rose Klix

Appalachian Fair Contest Coordinator - Rose Klix

Johnson City Sesquicentennial contest Coordinator Rose Klix
Poetry Day Proclamation Coordinator - Rose Klix

PAST PRESIDENTS PST-NE
PST-NE Branch founded Feb 2010

President - Rose Klix - Feb 2010 - Sep 2013

Co-Presidents Hugh Webb and

Chrissy Anderson Peters Oct 2013 - Apr 2014

Todd Bailey - May 2014- Apr 2015

J. Michael Ramey - May 2015-Apr 2016

Gretchen McCroskey - May 2016- Apr 2018

Rose Klix - May 2018-Apr 2020

OFFICERS PST KNOXVILLE 2019-2020

President Sharon Mishler Fox

Vice-President Ann Thornfield Long

Secretary/Treasurer Kay Fields

PAST PRESIDENTS PST Knoxville

President, Sharon Mishler Fox, 2018-2019

PAST PRESIDENTS

Raymond McCarty	1953-54	Charlie W. Sturm	1954-55
Gordon Lockhart	1955-56	Louise Malone Ross	1956-57
Anna Gordon Dean	1957-58	Walter Chandler	1958-59
Lillian Terry Harrison	1959-60	Anna Gordon Dean	1960-61
Patricia Murphy Reber	1961-62	Walter Chandler	1962-63
Gordon Lockhart	1963-65	Lucille D. Short	1965-66
J. Pat Babin	1966-68	Robert Simonton	1968-70
Frieda Beasley Dorris	1970-72	Dr. Rosemary Stephens	1972-74
Bee Bacherig Long	1971-76	Ann Carolyn Cates	1976-77
Jerry Leo Robbins	1977-79	Chester A. Rider	1979-81
Kenneth D. Thomas	1981-83	Dr. Wanda A. Rider	1983-84
Robert Simonton	1984-85	Elizabeth Pell	1985-86
Lula May Adams	1986-87	Frances Brinkley Cowden	1987-89
Thomas McDaniel	1989-90	LaNita Crouch Moses	1990-91
Ann Carolyn Cates	1991-92	Ruth Thomas	1992-93
D. Beecher Smith II	1993-95	Dr. Diane M. Clark	1995-97
Patricia Smith	1997-99	Russell H. Strauss	1999-01
Frances Brinkley Cowden	2001-02	Nellie H. Jones	2002-03
Michael R. Denington	2003-05	Russell H. Strauss	2005-07
Michael R. Denington	2007-08	Russell Strauss	2008-10
Sarah Hull Gurley	2010-11	Randall Stoker	2011-13
JoAn Howerton	2013-15	Russell H. Strauss	2015-16
Leslie Blakeburn	2017-18	JoAn Howerton	2018-19

THE HISTORY OF THE POETRY SOCIETY OF TENNESSEE

Charter of Incorporation: The Charter of The Poetry Society of Tennessee was granted June 30th 1953. Prepared by Margaret B. McCarty, Charter Member.

Founders: The seven signers of the charter are the founding members. At the second general meeting on June 20th 1953, these members were elected as the first officers of the new organization. Their names and offices ae as follows:

President – Raymond McCarty
Vice-President – Charlie W. Sturm
Recording Secretary - Inez E. Andersen
Corresponding Secretary – Cleo John Fox
Treasurer – Margaret B. McCarty
Directors – Kenneth L. Beaudion and Gordon Lockhart

Purpose: According to the Society Charter, the organization was constituted "for the purpose of bringing into being a close comradeship and mutual working fellowship among the recognized poets of the state; stimulating the as yet unrecognized poets of the state to make an effort for recognition in the established channels of expression; sponsoring the recognition of poetry as a creative art in the educational institutions within this state by encouraging the youth of Tennessee to secure the cultural background and appreciation necessary to achieve stature as a poet; and assisting and encouraging in every way possible the development of creative talent in the field of poetry."

Meetings: Regular meetings are at 2 pm on the first Saturday of each month excluding June, July, August, and October (Mid-South Poetry Festival). Since January 2013, the meetings have been held at the White Station Public Library.

POETS LAUREATE

Inez Elliott Andersen	1975-76	Charles Stanfill	1976-77
Raymond McCarty	1977-78	Eve Braden Hatchett	1978-79
Robert Simonton	1978-79	Frieda Beasley Dorris	1979-80
Bee Bacherig Long	1980-81	Chester G. Rider	1981-82
Kenneth L. Beaudoin	1982-83	Kenneth Thomas	1983-84
Mildred Boydston	1984-85	Carrie Sharpe	1985-86
Ann Carolyn Cates	1986-87	La Nita Moses	1987-88
Dr. Malra Treece	1988-89	Frances Brinkley Cowden	1989-90
Isabel Joshlin Glaser	1990-91	Thomas McDaniel	1991-92
Helen Allison	1992-93	Lucile Byrd Pitchford	1993-94
Norma W. Young	1994-95	D Beecher Smith II	1995-96
Louise Gearin	1996-97	Dr. Diane M. Clark	1997-98
Dr. Rosemary Stephens	1998-99	Patrick W. Smith	1999-00
Nellie Jones	2000-01	Russell H. Strauss	2001-02
Florence Bruce	2002-03	Harold Baldwin	2004-05
Michael R. Denington	2004-06	Malu Graham	2006-07
Elizabeth Pell	2007-08	J. Pompford Harris	2008-09
Sarah Hull Gurley	2009-10	Angela Logsdon	2010-11
Rose Klix	2010-11	Jeanine Mah	2011-12
Leslie Blackburn	2012-13	Caroline Sposto	2013-14
Randall Stoker	2014-15	Llewellyn Brawner	2015-16
Prince McLemore	2016-17	Charles Firmage	2017-18
Janet Qually	2018-19	Lori Goetz	2019-20

HONORARY MEMBERS

Florence Cogburn LeCoq	1955-56	Nora Johnson Cantrell	1955-56
Robert Sparks Walker	1959-60	Jane Merchant	1960-61
Paul Flowers	1962-63	Ollie Barnes Dayton	1964-65
Clarice Riddley Kelso	1964-65	Gordon Lockhart	1965-67
Inez Elliot Andersen	1972-73	Kenneth Lawrence Beaudoin	1972-73
Charlie Weddle Strum	1975-76	Margaret B. McCarty	1976-77
Raymond McCarty	1976-77	Ercil F. Brown	1983-84
Claudia Watson Stewart	1983-84	Margaret Gordon Williamson	1983-84
Bee Bacherig Loong	1984-85	Lucille D. Short	1985-86
Frieda Breasley Dorris	1988-89	Eve Braden Hatchett	1988-89
Corinne Frierson Hughes	1988-89	Helen Thomas Hughes	1988-89
Robert Simonton	1994-95	Dr. Rosemary Stephens	1994-95
Kenneth D. Thomas	1994-95	Lorraine Smith	1997-98
Dr. Malra Treece	1999-00	Frances Brinkley Cowden	1999-00
Thomas McDaniel	1999-00	Dr. Diane M. Clark	1999-00
Patricia W. Smith	2004-05	Michael R. Denington	2008-09
Ann Carolyn Cates	2010-11	Elizabeth Pell	2010-11
Russell H. Strauss	2011-12	Randall Stoker	2011-12
J Pompford Harris	2011-12	Florence Bruce	2015-16
Sarah Hull Gurley	2015-16		

THE 2018 MID-SOUTH POETRY FESTIVAL

The 2018 Mid-South Poetry Festival met at Leslie Blakeburn's home for a delightful potluck dinner and wonderful fellowship with fellow poets, guests of fellow poets, and a get acquainted with our workshop leader.

Jerry Hardesty was our guest workshop leader primarily centered on performance poetry. She gave everyone an opportunity to read their own poetry with tips on performing their own poetry. This workshop focused on bringing life to readings of their own poetry through open mic experiences, or other public events.

She is the founder, CEO, and Editor-in-Chief of the nonprofit, New Dawn Unlimited, Inc. (founded 1997), dedicated to poetry publishing, production, performance, promotion, preservation, and education. She enjoys different genres, from sonnets to slam, from haiku to epics, from sestinas to free verse. She served as President of the Alabama State Poetry Society and has been a speaker and workshop leader at poetry conferences around that area. Though she has her publishing company, she still manages to write her own poetry and has two chapbooks to her credit.

Instead of the meeting being held at the Holiday Inn, we utilized Southwest Tennessee Community College auditorium. We are blessed to have William Hill as a member, and he and his wife, provided continental breakfast items, and a bountiful lunch made by his lovely wife, Anna. It should be: We are blessed to have William Hill as a member. He and his lovely wife, Anna, provided continental breakfast items, plus a bountiful lunch.

Following lunch, contest winners were announced by Russell H. Strauss. We are always proud of those who continually support and submit their poems from year to year not only from Tennessee but various other states.

Special thanks to Lori Goetz for her outstanding assistance as my contest coordinator and her willingness to take on such a task. Also, a very heartfelt thanks to Marilyn Denington for sponsoring the "Best of the Fest" in memory of her husband. Last but not least, to all of our sponsors of the contests from year to year. Without you, this would not happen.

JoAn Howerton, Festival Director

WINNERS OF THE MONTHLY CONTEST

September 2018 Contest
Subject: Any
Form: Rondeau
Sponsored and Judged by Florence Bruce

Winners:
1st — Janet Qually, Memphis, TN — Angelic Jubilation
2nd — Barbara Blanks, Garland, TX — The Seeds of Love
3rd — Lynnie Mirvis, Memphis, TN — How Good It Is

ANGELIC JUBILATION

The angels sang from Heaven's height
when I was born anew one night.
My strength was spent; joy gone astray;
until I heard a preacher say
that God forgives and make things right.

Acknowledging my tragic plight,
I chose His path of hope and light.
As soon as I began to pray,
the angels sang.

My heart rejoiced when all its blight
completely disappeared from sight.
My soul now feels no disarray —
my faith is strong throughout each day.
When Love reached down and held me tight,
the angels sang.

November 2018 Contest
Subject: Any, but must contain at least 5 different colors; get out that thesaurus and be descriptive (don't use just red, blue, green, etc.)
Form: Any
Sponsored and Judged by Lori Goetz

Winners:
1st – She Sings Her Blues in Shades – Russell Strauss, Memphis, TN
2nd – Colorless – Von S. Bourland, Happy, TN
3rd – After the Rain – Barbara Blanks, Garland, TX

She Sings Her Blues in Shades

In a joint at a Delta crossroads,
beneath the jungle green tongues of kudzu,
she moans, azure as the afternoon sky,
while smoke from dozens of cigarettes
curls the tips of her notes to teal.
When darkness descends to cover
the white bolls of autumn cotton,
she wails to indigo, her voice,
diving into the shadowy shoals of human grief.
Sometimes she adds a trace of Latin lament,
as turquoise drips from her tongue,
but in the late, raven hours,
just before the crimson burst of dawn,
her songs sink deep into navy,
deeper than the ocean of night,
deeper than the depths of despair.

December 2018 Contest
Subject: Holidays
Form: Shakespearean Sonnet
Sponsored by JoAn Howerton; Judged by Crystal Robbins

Winners:
1st — Coming Home for Thanksgiving, 1963, Russell Strauss, Memphis, TN
2nd — Seasoned Love, Pete Harris, Memphis, TN
3rd — Holiday Unwrapped, Rose Klix, Johnson City, TN
1st HM — Easter Sonnet, Florence Bruce, Memphis, TN
2nd HM — Sharing the Season, Barbara Blanks, Garland, TX

Coming Home for Thanksgiving, 1963

The water towers, strung with Christmas lights
anticipate a season not quite here
On this, as on so many autumn nights,
shorn fields proclaim the dwindling of the year.
Perhaps I should be thankful for this bus
that sputters down an early-darkened road
toward where lonely "I" can melt to "us"
as stories of our family unfold.
On earlier Thanksgivings spent at home,
I thanked God for abundance. I still do
but now that circumstances make me roam
I thank God more that I will be with you.
May haloed stars proclaim their joy above
to light my way as I return to love.

January 2019 Contest
Subject: Any
Form: Any
Sponsored and Judged by William King

Winners:
1st — Russell Strauss, Memphis, TN — Fleeing the Blight, 1846
2nd — Barbara Blanks, Garland, TX — We Can't Let It Go
3rd — J. Pompford Harris, Memphis, TN — Fool's Goal

Fleeing the Blight, 1846

Before the thatched cottage
overlooking fields black with fungus,
he kisses his mother,
embraces his father.
Death hovers on the wind.
This year, pestilence and disease
have often knocked on village doors.
He slings his bundled clothing over his shoulder,
promises to write often,
promises to send money home,
promises someday to return,
but they all know the truth.
On the streets of New York,
he will fetch and haul
until his back cries from the burden
of being an unwanted stranger in a distant land.
He will earn enough to eat, perhaps to marry.
He will never earn money to travel.
Already, a million Irish have left, never to return.
As his figure fades down the pebbled lane,
his parents begin to weep
for a son they know they will never see again.

February 2019 Contest
Subject: Any Elvis Song
Form: Any
Sponsored and Judged by Russell Strauss

Winners:
1st — Charles Firmage, Eagle Pass, TX — To Tammy from Fred (inspired by Are You Lonesome Tonight)
2nd — Barbara Blanks, Garland, TX— A Fool and Her Honey Is Soon Departed (inspired by Devil in Disguise)
3rd — Sara Gipson, Scott, AR — Burning Love (inspired by Burning Love)
1HM — Rose Klix, Johnson City, TN — Peace in the Mountains (inspired by Peace in the Valley)
2HM — Lori Goetz, Germantown, TN — Mail, Always Welcome (inspired by Return to Sender)

To Tammy From Fred
("Are You Lonesome Tonight" by Elvis Presley)

WNEW radio from New York City takes requests.
"And this goes out to Tammy from Fred,
'Are you Lonesome Tonight.'" Another Saturday
night and Fred's staying home, plotting
plane geometry. He wonders if Tammy is listening.

His high school team wins again as Tammy waves
pom-poms, does flips, and dates the football team.
Cokes, Corvettes, pep rallies, and proms,
while Fred stays home, right by the radio.
"And this goes out to Tammy..."
Invisible Fred sits six desks behind her
in home room. If only he were captain of the team
or had a sports car, but he drives a Bug and plays
chess. He closes his eyes as Elvis sings,
"Are you lonesome tonight, do you miss me

tonight, are you sorry we drifted apart?"
He wonders if Tammy is listening.

It's the thirty-year class reunion.
The band plays as Tammy dances
with the former football players. She's now
a high-priced divorce attorney in New York City,
living alone in a condo with five cats;
never married.
It's Saturday night and the oldies radio station takes
a call, "And this is dedicated to Tammy..."
Fred wonders if she is listening.

March 2019 Contest
Subject: Any
Form: Blank Verse
Sponsored and Judged by Janet Qually

Winners:
1st — A Perennial Story, Barbara Blanks, Garland, TX
2nd — Fifth Grade Orator, Russell Strauss, Memphis, TN
3rd — Trading Places, Florence Bruce, Memphis, TN

A Perennial Story

She stood in church, evocative bouquet
of prairie roses clutched against her chest.
Ironic symbolism she supposed.
She wondered what had gone awry with him
since they began as such a perfect match.

Intrigued and captivated by a yard
replete with blooms as pink as lemonade,
she'd stopped, inhaled the color and the scent.
His eyes, of course, were focused on his phone.
He bumped against her, saw her glowing face;
impulsively he stooped and picked a bunch
and offered them in shy apology.

A nearby coffee hot spot hosted their
impromptu date. A year of flowers traced
seduction's path-she followed as he wooed
her: Picnic blanket sprinkled with a host
of dandelions- twirled beneath her chin
before his lips spread kisses, butter soft,
against her lips; chrysanthemums and phlox
corsage their plans for life together, while
a fete of purple pansies set ablaze

their passion, scorched and melted winter frost.

Now, here it was-sweet, blooming spring again.
He never showed-just pulled up roots and ran.
She wished the stems of her intensely pink
prolific flowers sprouted thorns, to prick
her palms, to stab until she felt a pain
that she could understand, to bleed from wounds
that weren't invisible, but vivid red-
not pink, not pink ... not prairie roses pink.

April 2019 Contest
Subject: Spring Surprise
Form: Any
Sponsored and Judged by Sarah Hull Gurley

Winners:
1st — Barbara Blanks, Garland, TX — Spring Rain
2nd — Charles Firmage, Eagle Pass, TX — My Name is Thomas
3rd — Gail Denham, Sunriver, OR — Spring Surprise
HM — Lori Goetz, Germantown, TN — March 1969

Spring Rain

Twirling in the rain is fun-
catching raindrops on my tongue,
water dripping off my nose,
squishing mud between my toes,
jumping puddles, splishing-splash!
Oh, I wish the rain would last.

But when a sunbeam mops away
the clouds, and shines a bright bouquet
of springtime colors in the sky-
I pump and swing until I fly
high as I can, then-it's so grand!-
I touch a rainbow with my hand.

If I could pluck each lovely stripe
and plant them-one of every type-
they'd festoon earth with brilliant blooms
to beautify all Heaven's rooms,
then shower petals down like rain-
and start the cycle once again.

May 2019 Contest
Subject: Any
Form: Any
Sponsored by PST-NE
Judged by Amy Jo Zook, Mechanicsburg, OH

Winners:
1st — "Upside Down World", Gail Denham, Sunriver, Oregon
2nd — "Walden Pond", Charles Firmage, Eagle Pass, Texas
3rd — "Perceptions", Barbara Blanks, Garland, Texas
HM — "A Great Way to Start a New Year?", Von S. Bourland, Happy, Texas

Upside Down World

Some days our world seems upside down
We long somehow to find a clown,
A crafty one to bring a break,
with comic moves; give us a shake.
We wish to end our constant frown.

We've blown our chance for a showdown
If we could keep the cheer that's flown.
We've worried long about what's fake.
On days our world is upside down.

What have we ever skillful sown
  that helps our country hold its own?
We've selfish acts for our own sake.
Some guides we've chosen to forsake.
Will we now let our country drown,
and watch our world sink upside down?

PATRON POEMS

Charles K. Formage

Nearest Place to Heaven

Elevators go up, others come down, constant
Opening and closing doors for thousands of office workers
Maintenance men, tourists, romantics new to town, and
Those who wish to reach
The observation deck to see where Cary Grant waited
In the movie, in the summer rainstorm, watching
Happy crowds getting off, milling about, looking out at the
City below, while he waited in vain for Deborah Kerr,
Until the last elevator took
Him down to walk the lonely streets
The Empire State Building's more than just
An office tower, more than just a tourist Mecca.
It's like a magnificent sundial, casting
Its long shadow across the city, effecting
The lives if New Yorkers and out-of-towners alike.
Once King Kong scaled its lofty tower,
Only to be attacked by bi-planes, but he wasn't
A native New Yorker, and his rough, ugly hands
Couldn't keep the girl, couldn't keep the beauty he desired.
The building's tower rides above the clouds on overcast
Days, like some floating
Space craft, hovering over a sea of cotton candy
Down on earth on the first floor, elevators stand ready for romantics who've made appointments
Months earlier to meet:
"If our love is true, we'll be there. If not,
There must be a darn, good reason." And so,
They flock here from Boston, from Seattle,
Even from Paris, France to take
The elevator all the way up to the 102nd floor,
Always looking up, as Deborah Kerr said in the movie,
"An Affair to Remember," to the nearest place to heaven
In New York City.

Rose Klix

Calorie Collection

Calories collect,
But not on my cupboard shelf
Or out of sight in the frig.
My stash isn't in my purse
But sits visible to the world:
On my waist, my thighs,
Under my arms and chin.
I'm saving, but forgot for what
Or which rainy day.
Now it's time to spend
Those calories at the gym

William Huettel

On Leaving a House Never to Return

All that is left is the light
From windows now undraped
That falls in sullen patches
On a bare and varnished floor
My footfalls make this hollow sound
That thuds down empty halls
And I am faced with finality
Now I close and lock the door
And this place and that part of me
That will never leave here
Quietly wait for dust

Gail Denham

Firestorm

Water poured from steel-gray sky
Buckets; fell in waterfalls. Firemen
in heavy yellow costumes clung to bulging
tan hoses strung from empty tanks, They
stood four abreast, spending all they had
to conquer nature's raging wildfire fury,
trying to save our homes.

Like hordes of locust, small red flames
Hop-scotched bush to tree. My small
Green garden hose sprinkled our roof
As if it had the lead in a major production
Yet all it could do was create lovely
Multi-colored rainbows, signs that beauty
Existed somewhere; forest glory taking
The back seat in this siege flames.

John Leslie Kolp

On John Leslie Kolp's Retirement

John!
Your life is a wilderness trail we must explore
Oh, the wonders you have brought forth for earth for all

John!
You are a flower in a world of weeds,
For people like you, we have great need.

John!
You have planted many seeds,
The trees whose deep roots hug stunning earth keeping dirt
in its place.
Soon all you have sowed will bud, bloom, grow.

Look!
There goes John trekking wondrous trails.
Hear echoes Italian dolomites, Swiss Alps
sing your praise

Heard John is in Austria gazing at a total eclipse
No, he is in Yosemite now, kicking up dust.
Yesterday, today, tomorrow, he will be refracting the Sun.
Whitewashing black tar roofs in the very scorching Sun.
We see Jon with a hoe in hand.
Oh street steward stopping invading killer species
To save many an urban garden from decay, misery, and rot.

There goes, John!
On the upper westside bicycling to keep the air fresh and
clean.
Heard John was in many streets protests marching for natural
causes.

One thing is for sure when it comes to earth,
John could not resist doing more.

And yes! There is, "N planet B."
Thank Goodness for your trailblazing shining light for saving us from urban blight

John!
You have left your mark too numerous to scroll here.
And when you depart this excellent earth,
Old street Steward, John!
We will see you in a natural habitat
The Sierra Club on the other side

And, yes!
We will sit and chat with George Washington, Abraham Lincoln,
Theodor Roosevelt, and Franklin D. Roosevelt, too.
And, we will talk about the world we once knew.

Vincent J. Tomeo

Roads Taken

Shake Paul's hand while Passing the Peace,
You'll grasp three straight-cut finger stubs,
Left by spinning teeth of a Craftsman circular saw,
He may still remember.

Melinda always sat on the right to the back,
Until with no notice last fall. Her Sunday family
Showed up to sit with two distant cousins.
The casket's grain pattern resembled a rabbit's ear.

A deacon got caught in the third deadly sin,
His wife sips tea with her book club as she decides;
His pals buy his coffee and biscuits at Shoney's,
Listening under their sports' talk-just in case.

Some say you can worship alone in nature,
Blacken unworn paths that bend through choirs
Of white trillium under evergreens,
Pray near a noble oak overlooking a pacific valley.

Instead I'll reach into the first century
For a think foot towel and a stoneware water basin,
Tuck in extra denaril for my watchful walk to Jericho,
Then stride in step alongside other pilgrims:

Take Pau to see Lowe's shiny John Deere mowers,
Sing Rock of Ages with Melinda's far-flung kin,
Watch Ron push around his hash browns with a fork.
On these paths I'll pray-then write my poem.

Calvin W. Ross 2018

My Muse Sings Only Country

My Muse sings only country,
Crying, dying, going somewhere
In a Juke-box beat.

I am
Roadhouse Homer
Honkey-Tonk Laureate
Singing to the rhythm
Of roaring engines
And humming tires.

I tease
Tears from
Good ole boys
Where waitresses are Didos
In a cross-country odyssey.

My Muse sings only country.

Boy By the Lake

A robin appears in front of my eyes,
The boy calls to his mother
He takes a picture of what he sees
Is it a fish or is it a duck?
A giant swan lazily drifts
The breeze gently blows on the lake
The boy photographs his mother
I sit beneath the shade of the trees
Snowdrop Anemone hides under the shade
A seed bud crabapple guards
Another ark covered tree.
As other children laugh in the distance
A spider crawls on my shirt and I kill it
Like the t-shirt I saw the other day

"We have nothing to fear but
Fear itself, and Spiders."
The dead spider's blood is on my hands.
Do I feel Buddist remorse?
No, the universe is too large,
To mourn the loss of a dead spider.
But a good haiku could give
the spider justice and immortality

Haiku
Oh, spider I knew
You crossed upon my shirt once
I'm sorry you died

WINNERS OF FESTIVAL POEMS

Benefactor's Award
Form: Any, 40 lines max
Subject: Any
Sponsored by Poetry Society of Tennessee
Judged by Budd Powell Mahan

Winners:

1-Sarah's Silence - Russell Strauss, Memphis, TN
2-Bird Watching -Florence Bruce, Memphis, TN
3-Route 77 to Globe- Barbara Blanks, Garland, TX
4-Aylan- Calvin Ross, Johnson City, TN
5- Last Maple- Janice Homburg, Johnson City, TN
6-Don't Wear Red While Sitting Outside with Birds - Fay Guinn, Jonesboro, AR

Sarah's Silence

Sarah never said the foolish things,
never ventured, "This is God's will,"
which we could not believe,
never offered, "He's in a better place,"
for there was no better place than with us.
Despite her three hundred pounds,
she dug holes in our pain
as noiselessly as a worm digging tunnels in loam.
For hours, she spoke not a word,
but the family, unable to sleep,
heard her breath in unison with theirs,
felt her heavy presence on the couch,
knew that she listened to their every lament.
Occasionally, she would rise to cover
a remaining child with a blanket
or to bring water to a coughing, red-eyed adult,
but she never spoke because there were no words
to comfort for early loss.
She finally rose at dawn
to fix breakfast for her family next door,
praying inwardly that she would never
experience the loss of one of her own children.
We, who are awkward of speech, still remember
the power of her compassionate silence.

2) Poet's Field Day Award
Form: Any, 40 lines max
Subject: Any
Sponsored by Poetry Society of Tennessee
Judged by Joe Cavanaugh

Winners:
1-Originals- Christine Irving, Denton, TX
2-Ready - Florence Bruce, Memphis, TN
3-Dragon to Kwan Yin- Christine Irving, Denton, TX
HM1-Abe- Christine Irving, Denton, TX
HM2-Park Encounter- Florence Bruce, Memphis, TN
HM3-All Night Vigil. . .Waiting for Fire- Gail Denham, Sunriver, OR

Originals

I want my favorite jeans to last forever.
I want the worn places on the butt
to keep sending signals, the way
a mule deer's white tail flashes
to tease the stag.
I wish the threadbare place
between my legs would reform
smooth and taut against my thighs,
that the knotted strings hanging from cuffs
would reknit themselves into straight seams.
I'll keep the blood stain from the climb up Devil's Peak,
the trace of ink where you scribbled, ' I love you'
and the three-cornered tear that my best friend Maggi
sewed up in the Arena bathroom
while the Stones were still on stage.
I never want those jeans to wear out.
When they do
I'm going to sew them in a quilt
with squares of wedding veil,
baby blanket, altar cloth,
dust cloth, dish cloth, rain coat.
They can bury me in it.

3) PST·NE Chapter Prize
Sponsor: PST-Northeast Chapter
Form: Any, max 50 lines
Subject: Any
Judged by Dr. Scott Honeycutt

Winners:
1-Eve's Apple Butter- Janice Hornburg, Johnson City, TN
2-Changeling- Tony Fusco, West Haven, CT
3-Going Home- Barbara Blanks, Garland, TX

Eve's Apple Butter

I do not need a serpent,
voluptuous globes seduce me.
I can almost taste the crisp,
white flesh on my tongue,
imagine kitchen's aroma of clove
and cinnamon, pungent scent of fall,
myself the country housewife
he always wanted.
I slither under the fence,
brave green briar, poison oak,
wasps drunk on fermented fruit,
to fill my sack with treasure.
At home, sink full of wormy
apples to pare, core, slice, spice,
stir the brown, bubbling lava
until sugars caramelize.
It splatters like hot grease
on tender fingers,
fills just two pint-size Mason jars
I could have bought at market
for a few dollars.
By the sweat of my brow,
tomorrow we'll eat home-made
apple butter, slathered
on hot biscuits- his smile
across the table, paradise regained.

4) Sarah Catherine Anderson Memorial Award
Sponsored and Judged by Sarah Hull Gurley
Form: Free Verse, 30 lines max
Subject: Shadows

Winners:
1-Shadow Dance- Faye Adams, DeSoto, MO
2-What to Leave for a Day- Catherine Moran, Little Rock, AR
3-Winter Miles - Lori Goetz, Germantown, TN
1-HM -In the Shadow- Lynnie Mirvis, Memphis, TN
2-HM- Unmarked Trails- Von Bourland, Happy, TX

Shadow Dance

Morning sun
captures windy breath
and a front-yard tree
outside my window
to shape a shadow dance,
mirrored on the grass.

Leaves flutter
like firework sparklers,
dancing in the sky
on the fourth of July.

Synergy of sun, wind
and spring-leaf canopy
unite to offer me
a jaunty greeting
on a sharp new day.

5) Perrie L. Knorr Memorial Awards
Sponsored and Judged by Diane Clark
Form: Any, 12-40 lines
Subject: Third Time's a Charm

Winners:
1-Stowaway, 1820- Russell Strauss, Memphis, TN
2-Last Kiss - Fay Guinn, Jonesboro, AR
3-Anniversary Charm - Sara Gipson, Scott, AR
1-HM- Personal Victories- Janet Qually, Memphis, TN

Stowaway, 1820

The first time, a second mate had discovered him,
tossing him from portside into a briny barrel.
The second time, his uncle had staggered aboard,
ranting in a voice thick from vodka
about the youth's ungratefulness as an orphan
toward family who sustained him with barley bread and
borsch.
This third time, a Baltic breeze
caught the sails that billowed like clouds
above a schooner that swayed gently as a cradle,
as land shimmered in a mist,
then faded into open sea.
The crew would find him, of course,
forcing him to earn his fare
by scaling masts and swabbing decks,
but he was an able lad,
free from his uncle's heavy hand
and on his way to fulfill his dreams
on the golden shores of America.

6) Winklebleck's Choice Award, in memory of Mary Winklebleck
Sponsored and Judged by Barbara Blanks
Form: Sonnet (traditional or variation), 14-16 lines
Subject: Any

Winners:
1-The Blues I Choose - Sara Gipson, Scott, AR
2-Absolution- Patricia Barnes, Wyandotte, Ml
3-A Sonnet for Sunday- Candace Armstrong, Murphrysboro, IL
1-HM- Polar-Jerri Hardesty, Brierfield, AL
2-HM- Elizabeth (Thinking about Robert) Just Before She Writes: "How Do I Love Thee ... " - Janet Qually, Memphis, TN
3-HM- Hot-Air Balloon Show Must go On!- Von Bourland, Happy, TN

The Blues I Choose
That lady sings her blues as if she's paid
her dues with life. To hear her voice, I've paid
the cover charge and donned a masquerade.

While trumpets chide and pump their soul for show,
I watch her arms and body sway and show
her vocal range surpasses most I know.

Her tapping feet imprint most every beat.
Her snapping fingers meet the pulsing beat.
My thumping thumbs repeat the drummer's heat.

I offer praise and toast by raising glass.
Her higher notes have shattered thicker glass.
Her raspy lows compete with sultry brass.

1 slide behind a masque to hide my heart
because divorce once split our life apart.

7) Missing Members Contest
Sponsored and Judged by Sarah Hull Gurley
Form: Any, Line count. ... You May Have To Ask ...
Subject: Any

Winners:
1-Roosevelt's Rondeau - Mark Hudson, Evanston, IL
2-To Beard or Not to Beard- Robert Schinzel, Highland Village, TX
3-An Island Love- John Crawford, Arkadelphia, AR
1-HM- Yesterday's Rose- Trina Lee, Oklahoma City, OK
2-HM - Greens of Spring - Sara Gipson, Scott, AR

Roosevelt's Rondeau

The 26th president was named Theodore;
scholars say he was the best.
He fought in the Spanish-American war;
and spent time exploring the west.

When he was done exploring on quests;
he served as vice-president before
President McKinley was laid to rest.
The 26'11 president was named Theodore.

He sent the Great white fleet on a tour,
through him America was blessed.
After the presidency he traveled some more,
scholars say he was the best.

African safaris were a thing, for which he had a zest,
he went to the Amazon, his health became poor.
With traveling, he had been obsessed.
He fought in the Spanish-American war.

His face is carved into Mount Rushmore,
and tourists visit the spot with great interest.
His spirit lived there forevermore,
and spent time exploring the west.

8) Triple Haiku
Sponsored and Judged by Lori Goetz
Form: Haiku (see instructions), 9 lines
Subject: Any

Winners:
1-humid pre-dawn heat- Christine Irving, Denton, TX
2-sleepless night- Janice Hornburg, Johnson City, TN
3-nocturnal mammal - Sandra Hancock, Big Sandy, TN
1-HM - a moonless sky- Janet Qually, Memphis, TN
2-HM - Ardent ivy clings - Russell Strauss, Memphis, TN
3-HM - Dead brown frosted lawn - Pete Harris, Memphis, TN

humid pre-dawn heat
summer's sauna cranking up
even frogs perspire

sunflower opens
petals sprawl like legs spread wide
to greet a lover

shrill cicadas trill
over-burdened branches droop
supine human naps

9) Hindsight Being 20/20
Sponsored and Judged by Lori Goetz
Form: Any, 24 lines max
Subject: Humorous advice to newlyweds or those planning to get married

Winners:
1-On the Toilet Training of Your New Husband- Russell Strauss, Memphis, TN
2-Eleven Syllable Epigrams for Engaged Couples - Janet Qually, Memphis, TN
3-Tit for Tat- Patricia Barnes, Wyandotte, Ml
1-HM- How to Succeed at Marriage Without Becoming Trying- Christine Irving, Denton, TX
2-HM -Advice for Slightly Off Couplets - Harvey Stone, Johnson City, TN
3-HM- Advice to the Lovely Couple- Jerri Hardesty, Brierfield, AL

On the Toilet Training of Your New Husband

Though some males find it difficult retaining
such basics, don't delay his toilet training.
There's nothing that will make a new bride fret
more than getting just-bathed buttocks wet.
Don't confront him daily or you'll rue it.
Repeatedly, he'll say," I didn't do it,"
nor does it help to steadily repeat,
"Dearest, drop that doggone toilet seat."
Smother him with kisses. Bake a pie.
Then, when your honey softens by and by,
tell your prince you find him truly charming
but just one trait remains that seems alarming.
Then, when your allurement has him hooked,
whisper," One more time, your goose is cooked."
Your Dr. Spock for spouses now has spoken.
Don't wait until your marriage vows are broken.
Don't fill him with new marital illusions.
Let him be a man and make conclusions.
You will be rewarded if you do.
He'll drop that seat just like you want him to.

10) Poetry Society of Tennessee- Knoxville Award
Sponsored by Poetry Society of Tennessee; Judged by Kay Fields
Form: Any, 30 lines max
Subject: Biographical poem, famous person or other real person

Winners:
1-Jackie's Prayer, 1963- Florence Bruce, Memphis, TN
2-Michael Paul Wilson (1911 -1 918)- Susan Maxwell Campbell, Mansfield, TX
3-Anne Frank's House- Nancy Lachance, Lebanon, MO

Jackie's Prayer, 1963

Holy Mary,
Chosen of God,
Mother of our blessed Lord Jesus,
help me!
If you were ever with me,
be with me now
and with my children.
Let me be strong and brave
as he was, for his sake,
for the family, for the nation.
Help me hold firm in adversity,
as he did, in spite of pain,
giving hope and courage to others.
Mold me into a sterling example.
Help me not think
about myself, my loss, until
proper respect has been paid established
protocols followed his
place in history fixed.
Be a sponge to soak up my tears;
be my staff so I don't stumble.
Calm the knocking of my knees.
Let the blood stains on my clothing
remind me of my duties here.
Keep my grief, which must wait,
a private thing.

Amen

11) Golden Shovel Award
Sponsored and Judged by Sharon Mishler Fox
Form: Golden Shovel
Subject: Any

Winners:
1-Ephemeral Dreams- Von Bourland, Happy, TX
2-Sky Time at the Cabin-Susan Maxwell Campbell, Mansfield, TX
3-Colossal Cogitations- Russell Strauss, Memphis, TN
1-HM-Tiger Dreams- Lynnie Mirvis, Memphis, TN
2-HM - The Gift- Patricia Barnes, Wyandotte, Ml
3-HM - Interlude - Barbara Blanks, Garland, TX

Ephemeral Dreams

What do I know of all
who circumnavigate my
sphere? What forms their days
consists of mystery. Are
their lives comprised of trances -
disappointment undermining and
controlling like a puppeteer? All
plans gone awry, much like my
own frustrations trapped in nightly
rope-wrapped-dreams?
My desires, my friends and loved ones, are
success each day where,
like a Midas touch, thy
golden gestures will bless each grey
tower in your broken dreams. The eye,
caught by the light, glances
then is held by beauty and
the mind follows where
that vision leads. May thy
pathway be paved with gilded footsteps
till it gleams
and you are engulfed in
glorious light. What
more could any seek, ethereal
though it seem, like rainbow-kissed bubbles? Dances
of joy might seem fleeting, but, by
grace and prayer we all may learn what
encompasses all things eternal
in heaven's holy streams.

End-words taken from:
" ... all my days are trances,
And all my nightly dreams
Are where thy grey eye glances,
And where thy footstep gleams In
what ethereal dances,
by what eternal streams. "
To One in Paradise---Edgar Allan Poe

12) Pat Smith Memorial Award
Sponsored and Judged by Florence Bruce
Form: Blank verse, 10-50 lines
Subject: Any

Winners:
1-Lusitania - Russell Strauss, Memphis, TN
1-HM-Liberating Something Positive- Janet Qually, Memphis, TN

Lusitania

Titanic brought an end to innocence,
but Lusitania led us to war.
The crew, aware that German U-boats lurked
beneath the waters of the Irish Sea
felt smug that speed could outpace submarines.
According to conventions of the time,
an unarmed ship must be approached and warned
and crew and passengers allowed the time
to take to lifeboats but Herr Schweiger's craft,
U-20, feared against so large a ship
their submarine would quickly be rammed down.
He launched torpedoes, blew holes in the side
and watched the ship immediately keel
to starboard. Then a new explosion rocked
beneath the funnels of a boiler stack.
The listing made the lowering of boats
impossible for many who would flee.
Though less than ten miles off the Irish coast,
the ship lost power and could not be steered.
Some lifeboats washed off empty from her decks.
while other spilled their cargoes in the sea.
Then power failed, and people trapped in lifts
could be heard screaming, pounding on the doors.
The captain of the ship, swept overboard,
somehow survived, when crewmen rescued him
unconscious from the raging winter sea.
Just eighteen minutes, that was all it took,
to sink her mighty hull into the depths.
Twelve hundred lost their lives that dreadful day,
civilian casualties of brutal war.
Titanic sank from error and neglect,
but Lusitania must bear the scars
of war's indifference toward innocence.

13) Western Women Award
Sponsored and Judged by Gail Denham
Form: Any, 32 lines max
Subject: Word Power

Winners:
1-The Master Is Served -Catherine Moran, Little Rock, AR
2-An Orphan Daydreams Catholic Wonders- Christine Irving, Denton, TX
3-Adventures of a Frontier Lady- Nancy Lachance, Lebanon, MO
1-HM -Wash Day Skirmish - Sara Gipson, Scott, AR
2-HM- The Sizzler- Barbara Blanks, Garland, TX
3-HM - Powerless - Russell Strauss, Memphis, TN

The Master Is Served

A nightly rat shinnies my bird feeder pole
and helps himself to sunflower seeds.

Cheese
was the first enticement.
He smacked it up every night,
but never snapped the trap.

Peanut butter
rolled into a little glob,
pasted on the spring,
was eaten with no results.

Payday candy bar
would tempt with peanuts
and sticky caramel.
All gone and he never
tripped the wire.

Chocolate cake
with dark icing
might do the trick.
It was gone the next day.

I imagine every midnight that black rat
takes out his pressed white napkin,
crawls over to the wooden trap in the grass,
and sits down to enjoy a prepared meal.
He nibbles around every wire and spring,
wiping his mouth with dainty satisfaction.

How carefully he feasts.
How deliciously he enjoys.
And the dutiful servant meticulously prepares
for the next night's spicy repast.

14) The Rondeau Contest
Sponsored and Judged by Von S. Bourland
Form: Rondeau, 15 lines
Subject: Any

Winners:
1-Maysa Gabriel- Fay Guinn, Jonesboro, AR
2-When Comets Fall-Jerri Hardesty, Brierfield, AL
3-She Loved You More- Faye Adams, DeSoto, MO
1-HM - I Love to Eat- Patricia Barnes, Wyandotte, Ml
2-HM- We Can't Let Go- Barbara Blanks, Garland, TX
3-HM- Reflection- Emory Jones, luka, MS

MAYSA GABRIEL

Her daughter sang with angel smile.
Though only twelve she had the style
of one beyond her tender years -
no guilt, conceit, or grown-up fears,
no ego, pride, performer's guile –

God's gift of grace in this great trial.
To honor life too soon defiled
by ravages of cancer's spears,
Her daughter sang.

Like broken bird this precious child
touched grieving hearts in pew and aisle
of sanctuary soaked with tears.
Air pulsed with music of the spheres.
Her mother's lifeless form lay while
Her daughter sang.

15) Dragon Dreams Award
Sponsored and Judged by Angela Logsdon
Form: Free Verse, 10-25 lines
Subject: Dragons

Winners:
1-It's Hard Being a Dragon - Gail Denham, Sunriver, OR
2-Survivor's Vow- Lori Goetz, Germantown, TN
3-Proper Cultivation- Trina Lee, Oklahoma City, OK
1-HM-A Dish of Dragons- Christine Irving, Denton, TX
2-HM - Dragon Defender- Russell Strauss, Memphis, TN
3-HM- The Grill of it All- Barbara Blanks, Garland, TX

It's Hard Being a Dragon

Blew too much; didn't mean to scare
or hurt the boy. My breath, always too hot,
no matter how much I drink to tone
it down or cool my inside furnace.

Hard being a dragon in this modem
day. People creep into my cave, search
for primitive wall pictures. I'm quiet,
take care not to hiccup or burp.

Must move deeper in the mountains.

Scary Big Feet back there, but they'll move
when I exhale. The rocky slopes where
I romped as a kid - dug up treasures.
Quarries, mines now in my rocks, my slopes.

Then there's food. Those humans
build more houses, cut down all trees.
The yummy high-reach leaves - gone.
It's hard, hungry, and lonely

being a dragon in today's world.

16) Do a Dutrey
Sponsored by Beverly Seaton; Judged by Florence Bruce
Form: Dutrey, 17 lines
Subject: Any

Winners:
1-Summer Song-Jerri Hardesty, Brierfield, AL
2-Elijah Waiting for a Promise- Von Bourland, Happy, TX
3-Biting Words - Sara Gipson, Scott, AR, TN

Summer Song

Summer bursts upon the scene,
Things with chlorophyll turn green,

Flowers bloom and bright birds sing,
Butterflies are on the wing,
Beautifying everything.
Growing grasses start to lean,
Busy bumblebees are seen
Tasting all the colored heads
Growing in the flower beds,
Yellows, purples, pinks, and reds.
Tubor, seed, and pod , and bean,
Vine and bud and in between,
Thriving, reaching, stretching out,
Doing what life's all about;
Count upon it with no doubt,

Summer bursts upon the scene,
Things with chlorophyll turn green.

17) Bobbie Drobeck Award
Sponsored and Judged by Russell Strauss
Form: Any, 10-32 lines
Subject: Interaction between people in two different age groups (example, senior citizens and young adults, adults and teens,
teens and toddlers, etc.)

Winners:
1 - How to Install a Zipper- Von Bourland, Happy, TX
2- Car Time- Fay Guinn, Jonesboro, AR
3- Sincerely- Faye Adams, DeSoto, MO
1 HM- Graft: Kisses and Roses- Susan Maxwell Campbell, Mansfield, TX
2HM- Lost Time- Robert Schinzel, Highland Village, TX
3HM - Waiting in Emergency- Gail Denham, Sunriver, OR

How to Install a Zipper

Take a girl whose mother is the ultimate seamstress could probably bake a cake with the sewing machine. Put that girl in a Home Economics class- too proud to ask her mother to teach her-or too nervous. For her project, choose a two-piece dress, red cotton with baby pink ribbon trim, tight skirt and sleeveless blouse with mandarin collar.

Take one red seven-inch zipper- follow teacher's directions for installation: "Read the instructions." Sew zipper into skirt. Inspect zipper. Zipper is upside down--cannot be unfastened at the waist. Take seam ripper, remove stitching, start over. Zipper flap is backward- from back to front, not front to back. Take seam ripper, remove stitching. Start over. Inspect zipper. Zipper is upside down.

Go home. Approach mother with head hanging low. Extend bag with partly mangled skirt. "!need your help. " Following a detailed explanation, Mother says, "Remove this zipper and throw it away. It is torn. We 'll have to buy a new one. "

Take one new red zipper. Open package. Read instructions. Mother throws instructions in trash. Panic! "You don 't need those. They're not worth the paper they're written on. " Under protest girl goes to the ironing board, allows mother to show how to pin zipper to skirt. Take skirt and zipper to sewing machine, stitch, and, voila! Zipper is not upside down! Zipper is not backward! Mother's baby girl is now a seamstress!

18) Animals We Love
Sponsored by Anna's Pet Sitting; Judged by Eleanor Berry
Form: Any, 16-32 lines
Subject: Animals we love

Winners:
1-I Have Served You Always- Susan Maxwell Campbell, Mansfield, TX
2-Moore, Oklahoma 2013- Nick Sweet, Shepherd, TX
3-Between Me and the Wild -Janice Homburg, Johnson City, TN
1-HM- Bodhisattva Dog- Christine Irving, Denton, TX
2-HM- Rival Attraction- Catherine Moran, Little Rock, AR
3-HM- Rough Start- Harvey Stone, Johnson City, TN

I have served you always

I have nibbled twelve springs' tender salads
(what are weeds for you), treed generations
of squirrels, stalked my share of cats (caught none),
and delivered three litters of pups — balls
of fluff, taken away one by one.
We've walked, you and I, in snow that demands
digging, through leaf piles where slimy things live,
and on softened blacktop roads in summers
that brought what you call "dog days"—not for me
when it's best to scratch in the cool damp earth
like a shallow nest under the porch.
My toes have clicked across the kitchen floor
to the same blue bowl you've always kept full
of fresh water. I no longer throw
myself down (always in your path), stretched full-
length to follow with my eyes your meal-time
to and fro. Now lowering this hip—
that sudden strange black car, your anguished face,
the evil-smelling cast, how you sat
on the floor by my crate as the vet walked
round you— hip I lower slowly
with a sigh to the plaid pillow (my place,
you call it). Doorbells and phones no longer
need my announcing bark; your guests still get
some wags, a good sniffing (What a sweet dog).
Now my delight is your bed — your odor
on the blanket, softness, an easy height
that needs no jump. You used to scold (No! Off!)
—it was all harmless. Now you stroke my head,
lift my muzzle to your cheek, nose to ear:
Are you dreaming of Heaven's squeaky toys?

19) Tanka Time
Sponsore
d and Judged by Janet Qually
Form: Tanka, 5 lines
Subject: Any

Winners:
1 - "if only" - Rebecca Drouilhet, Picayune, MS
2 - "bridal procession" - Russell Strauss, Memphis, TN
3 - "windmill blades turn" - Florence Bruce, Memphis, TN

If only
I could reach the stars ...
the child in me
climbs the first rung of a ladder
that used to scrape the sky

20) A Night with Shakespeare
Sponsored by JoAn Robbins Howerton and children; Judged by Crystal Robbins Czerwinski
Form: Shakespearean Sonnet, 14 lines
Subject: Anything to do with Shakespeare (interview, attending a performance, reading his works, etc.) with a love theme in it

Winners:
1-One of the Bard's Masterpieces: Romeo and Juliet- Janet Qually, Memphis, TN
2-Just a Coincidence- Jerri Hardesty, Brierfield, AL
3-Inquiring into Shakespeare's Love Life - Russell Strauss, Memphis, TN

One of the Bard's Masterpieces:
Romeo and Juliet

My feelings are as sad as they can get
since I read through a tragic Shakespeare play.
I want this mood to suddenly reset
and make it possible for me to say:

The lassitude affecting me is gone.
I've banished darkness to a distant place
where it will disappear and not hang on
corrupting any fresh, enlightened space.

A strong desire to write grows in my chest,
and so I grab some paper and a pen
in hopes that flowing lines, like William's best,
will come to be, and I can smile again.

Since Shakespeare's work is deeply touching me,
my theme shall deal with love and destiny.

21) Joan T. and Sheron B. Strauss Award
Sponsored and Judged by Russell Strauss
Form: Rhymed and Metered, 10-32 lines
Subject: Popular music (songs, songwriters, singers, musical trends, etc.)

Winners:
1-Rock Concert- Jerri Hardesty, Brierfield, AL
2-Walkin' with "Fats" Domino- Von Bourland, Happy, TX
3-Saxophone Blues- Sara Gipson, Scott, AR
1-HM - Light Jazz- Janice Canerdy, Potts Camp, MS

Rock Concert

Oh, give me hard rock lead guitar,
The melody will take me far,
Then add some driving bass and drums
With feedback squeals and reverb hums,
And once I'm really feeling fine,
Then scratch those strings right up my spine
To drive me crazy, make me dance,
And sway my hips in rhythmic trance,
But don't stop now, the power chord
Will captivate the cheering hoard,
Then bring it home with final verse
That shakes the very universe
And leaves me with my spirit high,
Yes, rock and roll will never die.

STUDENT WINNERS

WINNERS: 2018-19 All winners, teachers, and families are invited to the awards Saturday, April 6 at 2 pm, at Colonial Park UMC.

ELEMENTARY SCHOOL, JUDGES: WHITNEY and KAYLEE WRIGHT
1st Thankful, Lindsey Massey, Grahamwood Elementary, Sherry Coates
2nd If I were in Charge of the World, Eden Emerson, Grahamwood Elementary, Sherry Coates
3rd As I Travel through the World of Shakespeare, Lindsey Massey, Grahamwood Elementary, Sherry Coates
4th Autumn, Yazmin Rueda, Shelby Oaks Elementary, Amelia Bogdal
4th Loneliness, Emily Dorian, Grahamwood Elementary, Laura Wilon
1HM Happiness, Gabriel Martin, Grahamwood Elementary, Sherry Coates
2HM Pygmy Shark, Grahamwood Elementary, Sherry Coates

MIDDLE SCHOOL, JUDGE: RUSSELL H STRAUSS
1st A Little Lily, Marissa Lu, West Collierville Middle School, Mrs. Davis
2nd An Elephant with Wings, Abbie Dungan, Mt. Juliet Middle School, Mt. Juliet, TN, Cheryle Scudder
3rd The Lonesome Fowl, Crews Gieselmann, White Station Middle, Karla Varriano
4th I Spoke a Single Word, Marcus Beebe, Mt. Juliet Middle, Mt. Juliet, TN, Cheryle Scudder
1HM Equality, Chitkala Alli, White Station Middle, Karla Varriano
2HM Time, Max Laumann, White Station Middle, Karla Varriano
3HM Ode to the Moon, Jonathan Mintz, White Station Middle, Karla Varriano
4HM The Glacier, Jacob Geiser, White Station Middle, Karla Varriano

HIGH SCHOOL, JUDGE: RUSSELL H STRAUSS
1st Ms. Rose, Jocelyn Strait, Germantown High, Billy Pullen
2nd I Hear the Kitchen Singing, Khai Cole, Germantown High, Billy Pullen
3rd "Can You Hear Me Now ?," Caitlun Smith, Germantown High, Billy Pullen
4th In the Heavens, Emma Ketchum, Germantown High, Billy Pullen
1HM I Speak in Diffraction, Elaine Fu, Houston High, John Traverse
2HM Amaryllis, Chloe Baker, Germantown High, Billy Pullen
3HM The Pugilist, Nicole Li, Collierville High, Sarah Newman

EYE-POEM WINNERS: JUDGES: WHITNEY and KAYLEE WRIGHT

ELEMENARY
1st In the theatre, Stephanie Garcia
2nd Just, Owen Opp
3rd Make your life, Francisco Puerto
4th On, Genasis Moseley
All winners are from Oaks Elementary, Amelia Bodgal, teacher

MIDDLE SCHOOL
1st   Inspired, Crews Gieselmann
2nd   Promote, Shania Moore
3rd   Kids, Nathan Gruber
4th   discover life, Logan Ahern
1HM The adventure, Garrett McNeill
2HM The, Sarah Cameron

All winners are from White Station Middle, Mrs. Karla Varriano, teacher

Division: Elementary

THANKFUL

I am Thankful.
I am the satisfied feeling after a comforting meal.
I am the whispered prayers of people who care.
I am the blessings you count.
I am the taste of a sweet cookie after a calm hike.
I smell like warm, gooey brownies baking in the oven.
I am Grateful.
I am Appreciative.
I am the emotion that makes you say, "Thank You."
I am the feeling you get at night just before you drift off to sleep.
I am the gratefulness that calms you in your hour of dread.
I am full of praise for the resources I have.
I am THANKFUL!

Lindsey Massey
Grahamwood Elementary
3950 Summer Ave.
Memphis, TN 38122
5th Grade CLUE/Sherry Coates

Division: Junior

A Little Lily :A double abecedarian poem

A lily sways in the breeze of fuzz
Blazing yellow with the sky.
Cadmium equinox.
Drizzled with specks of dew.
Every sway of improv
Frizzes her hair and lifts her tutu.
Giving her a quaint
Hazy look. Harmonious
Inside that chamber
Jewels float in an umiaq.
Killing the eye like a sunlamp
Leaving a scar from her volcano
May her life be unfrozen,
Nymph of the kingdom.
On the soft petal
Pushes a lark
Quite the reminder of when she could conju-
Re the hum of a timpani.
Sits a bee on a bypath
To the state of giving
Under her beauty and glamour, itself,
Veiled, is a heart of tough jasmine
Which sprinkled
Xenical courage to all vivify
Youthful flowers who had succumb.
Zephyrs whistle in lily's zeriba.

Marissa Liu
West Collierville Middle School
1101 N Byhalia Rd
Collierville, TN 38017
Grade 8 /Mrs. Davis

Division: Senior
Ms. Rose

The smoke entwined with her perfume,
Sharply twisting and turning,
Giving off a putrid smell.
She loved those god-awful cigs.
She would sit in her large armchair,
Her overbearing body filling
Every crevice of velvet with her silk dress.
Puffing, huffing that god-awful cig.
Her smirk full of sarcasm and sass.
If you gave her even one long look,
She'd say "you ever seen a large woman hun?"
She loved those god-awful cigs.
You could often find her staring,
Longingly at the skinny women on TV.
Not knowing she held beauty,
Puffing, huffing that god-awful cig.

Jocelyn Strait
Germantown High
7653 Old Poplar Pike
Germantown, TN 38138
12th Grade/Mr. Billy Pullen

THE EYE POEM was invented by Kenneth L. Beaudoin (1913-1995) one of the founders of the Poetry Society of Tennessee.

In an Eye Poem, you create a poetic collage using visual and verbal imagery.

A free verse poem is constructed by combining images from magazine pages with words, phrases and clauses to create a poem on one page. The objective is to create a mood or inspiration. Do not write a poem first and then look for pictures. The poem is a discovery of words that fit with the graphics. You should be able to read the poem three feet away.

Find a picture or pictures up to 8 1/2 x 11 inches. Vertical is best. Go through one or more magazines and find words or phrases etc. that remind you of the graphics (pictures). Cut the words out neatly and place on the page of graphics. Do not use words smaller than 14 font. LARGE WORDS will be read louder and have more emphasis.

Do not cut out letters to make a word. Position the words and images on the page; if the Eye Poem will be submitted for contests, publication, or will be framed, keep a border of white space around the poem so that no words or images are cropped during production/publication.

www.ingramcontent.com/pod-product-compliance
Lightning Source LLC
Chambersburg PA
CBHW020145130526
44591CB00030B/225